Choosing the Best Coding Bootcamp for You

Insider Stories, Application Checklist, and Career Tips

David Kim

Acknowledgement

To all who aspire to learn to live a fuller, happier life. To those who help others do the same.

Table of Contents

Introduction

So you want to become a computer programmer? You decided to make a guided transition and gain the necessary skills to get a software engineering job. You've heard much about these coding bootcamps. What exactly are they? And will it help you launch your engineering career? What's hype and what's not?

If you are early in your decision-making process, you might be excited and overwhelmed. The idea of taking a big step and joining an immersive coding program can be exciting. At the same time, the decision may scare you.

It is a big leap to quit your job to enroll in a full-time Coding Program. Should you take the plunge? The decision can be expensive and disruptive. And you might be asking: will I have a job after I graduate? How good a developer will I become after a full-time program? Couldn't I just learn to program on my own?

I met Kevin for lunch at a San Francisco neighborhood sushi joint (inner Sunset, if you're curious). He was considering moving to the East Coast for a few months to stay with his parents while learning to code. His dad was a professional programmer, and Kevin was optimistic that he can make good progress on his own. Why was he going it alone? The main reason was that it was just so darned expensive to attend a bootcamp. Plus, the program of his choice was 12 weeks long. He figured he might be wasting some time going over the basics when he'd already gone through it.

A few months later, I checked in with Kevin. He was still doing well, but he wrote to me: "It's a lot harder than I thought." He was keeping things in perspective and using other resources to make progress, but it was still hard. Another few weeks later, he said he was returning to San Francisco later in the year to attend Dev Bootcamp.

I wrote this short book to help you and people like Kevin.

I will show you how to prepare for applying. I also share experiences from alumni, who offer valuable insights in their own words. With so many bootcamps out there, it may be difficult to find which program best fits you.

There are many online tools today to help you compare different bootcamps. So, I want to focus on information that will help you clarify what kind of experience you want.

I want to focus on sharing relevant information that will prepare you for the best program for you.

Along the way, I will suggest some helpful exercises to help you reflect on key questions. I will also share useful resources to save you time and money.

The bottom line is, you'll be better informed before you make a big life decision. Information is power.

I was among the early team members at Hack Reactor. In that capacity, I got to see the inner workings of a premier coding bootcamp. Moreover, I got to know other coding bootcamp leaders around the Bay Area. I met people who started App Academy, MakerSquare, CodePath, and so forth. I got to see which student did well and which didn't. I gained first-hand insight into what made one coding bootcamp great and another mediocre. On the online front, I consulted for Code School.

The students who read this book found it helpful in making their decision about whether to pursue the path of entering a bootcamp. And I want to go one further and offer some career advice. I will touch upon how you can prepare for and negotiate the best start for yourself. I believe this small investment of your time and money will pay huge dividends. So, I hope you'll pick up this book if you are considering a coding bootcamp.

Who is This Guide For?

This guide is for those learning web development. This guide is for those considering an immersive coding education. This guide is for those looking for more information on coding bootcamps.

Remember. Only you can decide what you want out of life! My role is to furnish you with constructive thoughts and useful information to help you in your decision. To that end, my goals are:

- Provide an overview of Coding Bootcamps
- Identify pertinent information to save you time and stress during research
- Introduce stories of other people who took the plunge
- Share career advice to help you jumpstart the job-search process
- Help you make a better decision about attending coding bootcamps

You are about to start on a fun journey. Do not sit back with this information; instead, actively engage it. Use it as a starting point for further inquiries. Keep learning to code while you apply. Keep learning other skills to expand your technical knowledge. Other questions should come to your mind. Talk to friends or reach out to people at Coding Bootcamps to further your research.

If you haven't already asked, *ask yourself why you want to attend a coding bootcamp.* Are you a career switcher? Are you seeking to add a skill to your existing portfolio? Do you want a convenient, and guided way to learn a new programming language? Are you enticed by the dream of becoming your own technical co-founder, and building the next famous startup? We'll dig into some of these questions.

You are reading this guide, because you want to be better informed about your decision. You do not want to spend next several months of your life and upwards of $12,000 of investment only to be unemployed, or worse, to regret your decision and still be uncertain about what you want out of life and career. That's why I wrote this guide.

Finally, this guide is a compilation of personal stories and insights. I believe hearing the stories of others who went before you can help you better navigate the terrain. I hope the stories and advice found in this guide will be useful to you, and save you time in your search.

As I noted, I had the privilege of working closely with coding bootcamp staff. I also had the opportunity to talk to many engineering hiring managers and recruiters. That's why I want to offer you some career insights in this decision making toolkit. I can share something unique and valuable with you. And this information is coming from an independent voice. While I once worked at Hack Reactor, I no longer do. I just want to empower you with information.

So, don't delay in reading through this guide. Gain important insights that will save you time and headache as you consider coding bootcamps. Most of all, choose the best program for you by taking the time to understand who you are and what you are looking for.

Paying It Forward

If this guide helps you, consider giving back. Please pay it forward by sharing your bootcamp experience with others via this brief survey. (For those reading print-edition, the survey url is http://goo.gl/j4ybAF.)

Your insights are valuable to those who comes after you! Thank you for sharing!

Thank You!

Thank you for your time and trust in picking up this guide. From time to time, I would love to share tips from tips to help you be successful in your career. I'll let you know about useful resources or workshops.

Please connect by tweeting @findinbay.

8

1. Basics: What is All the Fuss About?

What is a coding bootcamp? A coding bootcamp is an immersive program for accelerating your entry into a programming career. Sometimes a coding bootcamp is called a programming school or a vocational accelerator.

In-person immersive programs are best known among such programs. That means that you learn in a cohort with your peers all day. Often, the duration of these programs are around 12 weeks in length. Some are shorter. Some are longer.

With the success of the early graduates, many programs have extended their offerings to online. For example, Hack Reactor and General Assembly (GA) now have both in-person and online offerings.

Some bootcamps started as an online immersive program from the beginning. For example, Bloc has always been an online alternative to in-person coding bootcamps. Meanwhile, companies like Udacity have focused on career training with programs like Nanodegrees. For example,

Udacity's "Front-End Web Developer Nanodegree" partners with companies like Github and Hack Reactor.

The key focus of many coding bootcamps is the successful launch of your technical career. That means, you can expect some part of the coursework to be about job preparation. Vocational programs want to prepare you for a career in software engineering. This is both good and bad. In a traditional university education, you have the time to scratch a few intellectual itches. You can let your mind wonder and wander. Such time could be fruitful. In a coding bootcamp, there is little time for leisurely exploration. Curriculums are often packed, fast moving, and you need to keep up.

Of course, the career focus is a spectrum. I spoke to a web immersive program director at General Assembly. I learned that GA does not promote its job search and placement as much as some other full-time coding bootcamps do. I learned that GA fosters an individual's desire for learning for the sake of self-improvement.

Marc Andreessen (creator of Netscape) has said "software is eating the world." The lost decade (the decade of economic malaise of the 2000's) has upended many traditional jobs. Many younger professionals feel there are fewer opportunities than in the past. Meanwhile, technological solutions to old problems are disrupting the traditional ways of doing business. No wonder that in this environment of confusion and opportunity, so many want to pick up what feels like the skill of the future.

It is no surprise that many people, from students to governments, are excited about coding bootcamps. Investing in high-tech education feels like a great idea.

Personally, I feel excited about this trend. I think that coding bootcamps complement and advance current educational opportunities.

That said, when it comes to your decision, I really want you to think objectively about who you are and what is going to be the best for you. Don't get carried away in someone else's excitement. Don't get carried away by other people's claims about how great coding is or how fun it is. You should *trust, but verify*.

Remember, this is your journey. You owe it to yourself to figure out what kind of programs work best for you. So, what are your options? What kind of coding bootcamp is right for you? Let's broadly consider the options. Vocational programming education takes many forms.

- FREE, in-person paths - An example is the Hacker School in New York.
- FREE, online paths - An example is Codecademy.
- Low-cost, online paths - An example is a Code School or Pluralsight subscription.
- Paid, in-person paths - An example is the App Academy in San Francisco.
- Paid, online paths - An example is Bloc.io or the Viking Code School.
- DIY - Do it yourself with books, projects, and mentors. Plus a lot of discipline.

Among the paid options, there are different ways of financing your education. See Chapter 6 for some ideas.

In an earlier edition of this book, I had listed some of the popular bootcamps in an appendix. Since the list is changing all the time, I think it is better to share links to online directories. I'll do that in an appendix.

Finally, keep in mind that you can get paid to learn. Find an internship or a job.

Alternatives to a Programming Career

A programming career demands constant learning. Depending on who you are, that can either be frustrating or fun. The thing about the act of programming is that it is a lot of fun. There I s an aspect of instant feedback that can be empowering and addicting. If you have built and deployed a webapp that has real users, you'll have a sense of what I mean. And if you are in a coding bootcamp, that kind of obsession with a cool project is common. And you are dying to post it on Hacker News.

Now, once you start work, you'll have to deal with more than just the fun parts of programming. In any job, you have politics and bosses who can't communicate clearly. You have stressful deadlines, lack of resources, and so on. And it can sap a lot of the fun out. The point that I am making is: don't glamorize the programming career. At least not yet. Once you've been through thick and thin and still love what you do, then power to you. I just don't want you making a bad decision just because you haven't thought things through.

The truth is, you may decide that a programming career is not for you. In that case, don't despair. There are many alternatives. To clarify, this is about alternatives to a programming career. There is an endless number of work you can do as a non-programmer even in tech. Rather than a long list, I want to share a story about a young lady named Ina. After Ina graduated from college, she had a choice of a stable job at a Fortune company.

Instead, she decided to pursue a startup job. To break in, attended a non-technical tech job bootcamp called Tradecraft. (Tradecraft has branches in San Francisco and New York.)

Ina shared her story on Medium. A short excerpt:

> *Dave Morin, Path co-founder and angel investor, was at the conference the whole day supporting his pregnant wife. Most conference attendees were young women, part of the maker movement, and not deeply involved with the tech scene - so they didn't recognize him.*

By taking the path less traveled, Ina learned all sorts of neat hustles. She ran into interesting people in tech, and made a huge impression on some. She learned the art of *creating her own luck!*

I won't spoil the ending. But, I suspect, Ina is going to be a huge success in tech.

If your dream is to break into tech and build interesting things, you could do so in ways other than writing the software.

Further Reading

- How I Hustled to Get the Perfect Job by Ina Herlihy

Chapter 1 Summary

- Understand the different types of education options - free and paid, remote and in-person.
- An internship or an entry-level technical job could be a great alternative.
- There are plenty of alternative tech career paths.

2. Unconventional Considerations

I know, I know. I didn't write this book to convince you not to attend a coding bootcamp. But, I really, really want you to be successful in whatever you do. So, I want you to take a level-headed view of the good, bad, and the ugly. Some of you who are considering a tech career may be thinking about it in the abstract.

Maybe you're in college, and you just see the best employer rankings. You see the prestige of working for a company like Facebook or Google. You know that the salary and benefits are going to be great, and the work likely will be interesting. Perhaps you are dreaming about a workplace that serves free artisan coffee and a fridge full of craft beer. Wait, a fridge stocked full of beer? At work? Is that a thing now?

Well, if you work in tech in San Francisco, artisan coffee and craft beer in the office is definitely a thing. While that's going to sound fantastic to some of you, it's going to remind some of you of not-so-fantastic times in college. Have you heard of something called the "brogrammer culture?" About 77.465% of all software developers are dudes, and depending on where you work, might be a lot of young dudes. (That's not a scientific figure, by the way. I'm just joking, but it's a lot of guys.)

Which is to say, diversity is a big issue in tech. The nice thing is that things are changing. For example, Buffer recently dropped the word "hacker" from its job descriptions. Let's be real. A lot of folks looking to get into coding full-time probably spend an unhealthy amount of time on Reddit threads and on Hacker News. Especially, hacker news. It's just part of the dominant culture. Yet, in the Buffer post on jobs, Buffer's CTO "noticed that Buffer was seeing a very low percentage of female candidates for developer jobs—less than 2% of candidates." Buffer doesn't disclose what the impact of changes brought. Still, it is clear that Joel, Sunil and his team want to be as inclusive as possible.

(As a quick side note, I met Sunil while at Hack Reactor. I'm pretty sure Sunil - like other CTO's - just care about finding the best talent who fit into the team's culture. Meaning, tech leaders are not intentionally alienating people. But, the reality is it can happen, and people are becoming more mindful.)

In an article called "Institutional Barriers for Women of Color at Code Schools," Stephanie Herrera talks about adversity and risks women of color face in coding bootcamps. In a related article, Shawna Scott talks about monoculture in tech and at Code Schools (full article link). As a one-time Startup Digest curator in Silicon Valley, I concur with some of these sentiments. Certain aspects of startup culture feel uniform and broken.

So, when you are thinking about career transition, or entering a coding bootcamp, it would help to think past yourself. Instead, imagine yourself in that environment and interacting with other people. Depending on the bootcamp, you might be working with a bunch of young guys. If you don't have a problem with that, that's fine. And even if you are not of the same demographic, things may be just great for you. All I want to make sure is that you've thought about it.

Cool? Now, I think we can finally get down to business and focus on choosing and getting into coding bootcamps!

Chapter 2 Summary

- Know who you are and know what you want.
- Coding bootcamp culture can be great for some, not so great for others.

3. Getting In: Researching and Admissions

If you read the information on a coding bootcamp's website, or subscribe to a school's newsletter, then you might grow weary of its superlative claims. Is it trustworthy? Who validates the claims, you might wonder. Well, no one. So, what to do?

I had a friend named Brenda. Brenda was interested in attending a coding bootcamp, but was unsure if she would be a good fit for the learning style at a particular bootcamp. Further, she was skeptical in the beginning. She wondered if she couldn't just learn it on her own and find a job. I suggested she visit the school and attend a lecture. By connecting with the bootcamp's leadership, she was invited to visit the school and spent a whole day during an early phase of a cohort.

Afterward, I asked her what she thought. She told me she was surprised by the pace. It was a lot more intense than she anticipated, and she didn't think she could learn what the students were learning on her own. A big veil of doubt was removed from her mind. She knew what the learning environment felt like, and she also knew that she wouldn't be able to learn "it" on her own.

Nevertheless, Brenda decided the bootcamp environment would not be a good fit for her. She knew she wasn't far from an entry-level developer position. She persevered in her job search and continued to work on her coding competency. In the meantime, the bootcamp administrators were impressed with Brenda's accomplishments, and told me she practically had a lock in on an admission spot if she wanted it.

Soon thereafter, Brenda had a job with an e-Commerce company as a front-end developer. In a way, she had her cake and ate it, too.

On Researching

Only two years ago, programming bootcamps were relatively unknown. Public information about them were limited. Now, bootcamps have mushroomed across the world. Information about schools has ballooned.

The purpose of the research should be to answer the big questions on your mind, so that you remove the unknowns. Doing so reduces the risks of your decision making. Now, everyone will have different questions. That said, I want to suggest some big questions in the appendix (see application checklist).

As a specific example, one of the things I would want to know if I am paying $14,000 is *how will this program help me learn awesome things and make me good?*" A better way to phrase that question is *"what is your school's unique approach or methodology to learning?"*

One of my friends, Erik Trautman, started an online bootcamp called the Viking Code School. Erik pointed out to me that he built his coding bootcamp with people who work in mind. Still, I wanted to know what made his program unique. Was he doing anything different from other coding bootcamps and their intensive teaching process? At Viking Code School, there is a strong focus on building a real product throughout the program. There is also a strong component of peer teaching and learning done through weekly Google Hangouts.

See how that small level of digging helps remove a layer of abstraction and give you a sense of what the program is about? That's what you'll want to do with programs you are interested in.

You might wonder, where do I find the information?

You could read guides like this one, or a similar guide by the Firehose Project. Such guides will give you a perspective and potentially inform your decision. If you would rather formulate your own opinions, you can use databases, a school's own websites, and read blogs from former students. (See the appendix to this book for a short list of great online directories of schools.)

You could also talk to alumni and ask about their experiences. This book incorporates a few alumni testimonies, but that's something you can do directly through social media. You will get some great perspectives and answers on Quora and Reddit.

Finally, you can visit the schools yourself and meet the instructors or see a class in session. I realize not everyone has this luxury to travel to the school. However, if you are in the area, I highly recommend an in-person visit. If you plan ahead, you can turn your visit into an opportunity to impress, as Brenda did in the above story.

To recap, here are some sources you can use to research a school and prepare for your decision:

- Online directories (see appendix)
- School's own websites
- Personal blogs/vlogs
- Books or brochures in print and online
- Quora - Programming Bootcamps topic
- Reddit - example thread
- Talking to your own network directly
- Site visits

About Admissions

In this section, let's hear from those who are on the admissions-side of the bootcamps. You may see two broad themes emerge on what it takes to get in: 1) you enjoy coding, and 2) you are a good human being.

I asked Michael Kaiser-Nyman, founder of a programming school called Epicodus (Portland, Oregon formerly in Sacramento, California). Michael is an alumnus of Dev Bootcamp and an all-around great guy. Michael shared:

> *I can't speak for any other coding school, but there are two things I look for in Epicodus applicants. First, they should have tried programming before, so that*

they know that they like it. Second, they should be a good team player.

Sean Daken, founder of RefactorU (Boulder, Colorado) looks for people with high general intelligence, emotional intelligence, and professionalism.

We want people who are passionate about the path they are pursuing, who have a sense of urgency, and who have maturity in spades. Successful applicants need to be able to communicate very well, be driven and willing to work hard, and be able to learn and apply new concepts quickly. Basically, we're looking at applicants through the lens of a hiring manager - smart, driven, passionate, very strong communicator, etc. We actually score applicants quantitatively and qualitatively based on perceived raw general intelligence, communication skills, professionalism, passion, how much they have invested up to the point of the application in learning on their own, etc. We determine the score based on a combination of their application responses, interviews, and in some cases reference checks.

Note Sean's highlighting of *soft skills*. Further, Sean gives nod to how employability plays a factor. Sean continues:

It helps to have some prior coding experience, but [it is] not absolutely required. It is important that people have tried to learn something related to programming on their own, not so much for what that is in particular but that it shows that they have taken initiative and are serious. The best candidates have all of the qualities I mentioned above AND have tried to learn as much as possible on their own. They know what they want and know that RefactorU is the most efficient path to getting them there.

Shawn Drost, a co-founder at San Francisco-based Hack Reactor lists the following key attributes during the admissions process:

- **Drive** - We want to work with people that will push themselves and their peers to surprising amounts of success.

- **Warmth** - The school ends up being like a family, and my cofounders and I go to crazy lengths for our students that don't make any sense from a business perspective. Life is too short to spend time with assholes, even when they're all-stars by other metrics.

- **Effectiveness** - It turns out that getting things done is a unique skillset that carries over between careers/environments. We like effective people - those skills apply just as well to software engineering.

- **Intellect** - Raw horsepower also matters.

- **Technical Chops** - Many intelligent people will never become software engineers, either because they don't actually have a deep interest in the field or because it just doesn't align with their mindset. We ensure that applicants have learned the first 10% on their own, mostly so that we know for sure that they can clear those hurdles.

Let's look at another source. Hacker School is based on New York. From its blog about What We look for in Students, one can find several attributes:

- You enjoy programming
- You want to get significantly better
- You are friendly
- You are self-directed
- You are intellectually curious
- You have a demonstrated capacity for rigor
- You are introspective

As you can imagine, a coding bootcamp learning environment is both intense and collaborative. This means that the satisfactory progress of everyone in a given cohort is very important to the teaching staff. If someone falls behind, that could jeopardize the quality of learning experience for others in the class.

Moreover, the caliber of your peers directly impacts the quality of your learning experience. Accordingly, when admitting a class of students, admissions staff pay close attention to how well you might learn together with others. Many bootcamps assess your ability to learn together with a two-step test.

The first phase is a non-technical conversation about your background and your goals. Next, you likely will solve a test problem or pair program with someone (remotely or on-site). At that phase, you should remember that how you approach collaborating is more important than getting the right answer. Of course, you should aim to do well in answering your question. But, what the admissions staff really needs to know is how well you communicate while you program. Do you logically talk through your process? Can you lead the pair in a manner that's both pleasant and intelligent? And lastly, this might give the admissions staff a chance to see how you react under pressure.

Knowing that agenda, one of the things you should prepare for is to have a plan for getting unstuck during pair programming. If you are totally stumped, what should you say? How would you ask your pair for help in a way that clearly shows you have thought through the problem, but need additional guidance?

At the end of the day, coding bootcamps are inextricably linked to the tech employment trends. Placement success is a key success factor for most bootcamps. Therefore, bootcamp admissions officers are ultimately keen to find effective people who did well in their past endeavors. People with energy who get things done, the thought goes, will be able to find a job once the program ends.

Chapter 3 Summary

- There are many resources for gathering independent facts about a bootcamp.
- You should make plans to either talk directly with alumni or visit a school on-site to get a real sense of whether you fit in.
- Admissions are typically based on two phase interviews following your application.
- First conversation is non-technical in nature: tell me about yourself type or why do you want to attend type of question.
- Second conversation is to assess your fit, often through a pair programming exercise.
- It is important to demonstrate both technical and emotional competence.
- Be prepared to get unstuck and show that you would be a model peer within the cohort.

4. The Art of Learning

Did you try something today and failed? How about in the last week? How about in the last month?

If you are struggling to answer this question, then I suggest you fail at something today. Like right now.

Why? Because learning is a process of failing until you unfail. You likely know about and read Hacker News. You may also know about its creator Paul Graham (of Y Combinator fame). In his book Hackers and Painters, Graham notes of his programming style:

> "*I tended to just spew out code that was hopelessly broken, and gradually beat it into shape. Debugging, I was taught, was a kind of final pass where you caught typos and oversights. The way I worked, it seemed like programming consisted of debugging.*"

I like that. Programming by debugging. The truth is, you're going to bang your head on the wall a lot while you learn to program. I learned from my friends that even experienced programmers frequently get stuck. This is the reason why you must learn to be patient with yourself and be disciplined about learning.

As Plato noted of Socrates, a wise woman knows that she knows little or nothing. According to Plato, Socrates noted "I know that I know nothing." Remember that Socrates was widely considered to be one of the wisest people ever to have lived.

Getting Unstuck

Certainly, you need to be comfortable with how little you know. At the same time, you must focus on incremental progress. If you think about the idea of programming by debugging, you are making progress one error at a time. One line of code at a time. Do you have that kind of patience?

> *"Success is the ability to go from failure to failure without losing your enthusiasm."*
>
> **Winston Churchill**

This is not to say you should celebrate being slow. Rather, successful programmers take productivity seriously. Some of that comes from becoming super familiar with the tools of the trade. Hence, you hear of heated debates between Emacs and Vim users. This is not just about being a geek; it is about being serious about the tools you use. Why? Because you want to be as fast and effective as possible.

At Hack Reactor, we used a phrase: "getting unstuck."

It meant remembering not to stay in the gutters too long. It is not unusual for a programmer (new or old) to spend hours tracing some tiny bug down the rabbit hole (or the database). If you are a student and you are on schedule, you needed a way to move on. What separates the pro from the amateur is that the pros know when to stop and ask for help. They are pragmatic, and know they can either ask another expert for help, or table the bug for later.

When you are applying to a program, make sure you ask what system is in place to ensure that you don't get stuck for too long. Does the program have a help request system and peer working sessions? And this is a powerful advice to take to heart. What is your own system for getting unstuck when you run into a hard problem in programming? In life?

Now, all this talk of failure - real or metaphorical - might be a bit of a downer. Don't despair! You are learning.

> *"If you want to increase your success rate, double your failure rate."*

> **Thomas J. Watson**

Well, at least Tom Watson knew what was up. (He founded IBM.)

Further Reading

- Why Learning to Code is So Damn Hard by Erik Trautman

Chapter 4 Summary

- Learn to embrace failures, so long as you are learning from them.
- Be patient with yourself. Learning is incremental; take small steps forward.
- But, don't get stuck too long. Reach out for help as the pros do.
- Don't let perfect get in the way of better.

5. Is It Worth It? The ROI

Should you get an MBA or learn to code? What is the return on investment (ROI) for a programming course?

Return on investment is a plain concept that both prospective engineers and business students can understand. The following comparison may not be a perfect apples-to-apples comparison, but don't miss the forest for the trees. Let's compare two scenarios:

- Option 1 - attend 2-year full-time MBA program
- Option 2 - attend 3-month full-time programming course

What are the invested costs and expected salary after the program? For simplicity, let's compare gross (before-tax) salary and expenses. Basically, cash in and cash out. We will leave the discussion about the intangible things like network or personal growth, etc. It's definitely relevant, but best left for a separate debate.

Get an MBA

Let's take a premier Business Schools - Harvard Business School (HBS).

Investment

Per HBS cost summary page, it costs a single person $95,000 per year to attend the school, all living costs included (for 2016 budget). That's close to $190,000 for two years!

Return

Salary for a business school graduate depends on the industry and company. Let's take highest median MBA salary from 2014 HBS Employment Report. That job is in private equity. Keep in mind, you will not have started working until three years after you start school.

- Summer internship salary for LBO/private equity (assume 3 months) - $24k
- Year 3 - median LBO/private equity salary year 1 - $150k
- Year 4 - let's assume a 10% bump with good performance in year 2 - $165k

So, here you are, 4 years after you first attended business school.

ROI = $339k / $190k = 1.78 or about 180%.

Learn to Code

There's not a strong or widely publicized salary data around this yet (so this is slightly an orange), and so I use a well-recognized industry report from Riviera Partners - a San Francisco based placement firm for tech talent. I can corroborate these figures based on indeed.com postings and also local tech group mailing lists where salary figures are thrown around ... so it's reasonable.

Investment

This varies by program from around $10k to $20k, but let's use an approximate mid-point at $15k for the program duration, which is generally about 3 months. You can read more about the schools and coding in a blog post - Soon your taxi driver may know more Ruby than you do.

- Year 0.25 - $15k
- Rest of year 1 – 0 tuition. You're making money if you are working
- Rest of year 2 – 0 tuition. You're making money.

Return

Salary figures, as noted are from Riviera Partners 2013 engineering salary review. Let's use a junior JavaScript developer.

- Year 0.75 - junior dev: $107k * 0.75 = $80k
- Year 2 - $112k (after a 5% raise)
- Year 3 - $118k (after a 5% raise)

A junior developer has 0 - 3 years of experience according to this report, so afterward you would be considered a senior developer.

- Year 4 - $124k (a senior JavaScript developer salary)

The reality is, many graduates from the 3-month program are hired directly out as an experienced developer.

Four years after you write your first lines of code at a school.

ROI = $434k / $15k = 28.9x

Beyond ROI

So which would you rather have?

This analysis is simplified. It might be too simplistic, but you are getting my point. My intent is to give the traditional education something to think about.

Financially, it might be a no-brainer. Do not make a decision only for the money. A fulfilling career is more than simply marking a buck. It is doing things you love doing, and about working with people you enjoy working with. That said, it's nice to get paid your worth. Isn't it?

Chapter 5 Summary

- The return on coding bootcamps can be big, exceeding even professional degrees like MBA.
- The opportunity cost of traditional models of education is huge when compared to the compact and speedy coding bootcamp model of education.

6. Financing Options

Suppose that you have decided to attend a full-time coding bootcamp. You know it's the right step for you. Even so, the price is an issue because tuition is expensive. What do you do?

In this brief chapter, I want to suggest some alternatives. I want to get you thinking about the possibilities. Don't end your journey simply because you believe you are unable to pay for a program.

While at Hack Reactor, I connected with a funding startup called Upstart to discuss using their platform to finance student educations. Sometime after I left Hack Reactor, I learned that the possibility had become a reality. Upstart now supports tuition financing for several bootcamp programs even if you do not have a 4 year college degree or a job.

I found other funding platforms like Puddle, started by former founders of Kiva.org, and Tilt.

More to point, these stories illustrate that there are different ways to fund your education. Where there is will, there often is a way.

So, beyond the tried and true method of saving up some money, here are some other ideas which may help you:

- Have your employer fund your education - this may seem far-fetched, but one of the first coding bootcamps was Living Social's internal training program.
- Crowdfund your education - it never hurts to have your friends and family pitch in, and it's a nice source of moral support, too. You have many options like Tilt and gofundme.
- Defer your tuition - some programs like App Academy has tuition deferral built into its business model. If you don't get a job, then you don't have to pay full tuition. (There is an up-front deposit to the program.)
- Borrow to attend - using services like Prosper.com or Upstart.com. (I prefer to avoid debt.)
- Free up your finances by consolidating prior student loans at a lower rate - using services like SoFi.

I wrote this section to help those attending a paid programming bootcamp. Keep in mind, there are cheaper or even free options. The price and format of the coding bootcamps will continue to evolve as the industry grows and matures.

If you would like to share your story of how you funded your education, please shoot me a note.

Chapter 6 Summary

- See Upstart's company website for a full list of eligible programs and eligibility requirements.
- There are a number of financing options, thanks to a slate of new online tools.
- Of course, consider how you can budget and save up first. Borrow as a last resort.
- Finally, keep in mind that some programs are inexpensive. Some are even free!

7. Alumni Profiles

Back in February of 2013, I hosted a panel event featuring 8 alumni from four San Francisco coding schools. It was a Q&A meetup event organized to help SF Ruby community members and prospective students ask questions of those who had been through the 'bootcamp' experience.

While I do not have the actual questions asked during that evening, I hope that the following stories and information will serve a similar purpose.

Would you like your profile featured? Please complete this survey: http://goo.gl/j4ybAF.

Now onto profiles. Each interviewee shared his or her experience in response to a set of prepared questions.

Coleman Foley, Hack Reactor in 2013

What is your favorite memory from the Program?

The day before I had to present my personal project to the rest of the class. It was a day off, and I spent the whole day getting my project as solid as possible for the presentation. It was really exciting to be able to make tangible progress quickly. At that point, I had been learning in the intensive environment of Hack Reactor for a long time, and I had been working on that particular project for quite a while, too, so I was able to make fast progress.

Tell us a story around your decision to attend. What were your goals?

I wanted to move from working in stores to a more professional career. I wanted to get more satisfying work. I expected Hack Reactor to speed me along that path.

And why did you choose your particular school?

It was longer and more intensive than the other programs, namely Dev Bootcamp. I liked its focus on the front end, too.

What were you doing before attending?

Fixing phones in a Sprint store.

What is #1 reason you would recommend your school to a friend?

You learn a lot faster than if you try to learn more independently.

What programming languages did the (official) curriculum cover?

Ruby & Ruby on Rails, JavaScript, CSS3/HTML5

Erik Trautman, App Academy in 2013 (San Francisco)

What is your favorite memory from the Program?

Seeing the increasing complexity of things I can build.

Tell us a story around your decision to attend. What were your goals?

I wanted to learn how to code to get a dev job and eventually build a business. I was learning on my own but it wasn't quite fast enough and I didn't even know if I was learning the right things.

And why did you choose your particular school?

The curriculum was heavily project focused but the primary differentiator was just the ability to get me into an early cohort.

What were you doing before attending?

Learning

What is #1 reason you would recommend your school to a friend?

Get an end-to-end context for becoming a web dev and work with other people along the way.

What programming languages did the (official) curriculum cover?

Ruby & Ruby on Rails, JavaScript, CSS3/HTML5

Michelle Glauser, Hackbright Academy in 2012

What is your favorite memory from the Program?

The moment my script worked the way I wanted it to for the first time was exhilarating.

Tell us a story around your decision to attend. What were your goals?

I just wanted to be able to build stuff myself. I'd always been interested in tech, and since my original career goal wasn't working out, I felt drawn towards programming.

And why did you choose your particular school?

I chose Hackbright because it cost less (at that point), it was women-only, and they let me in.

What were you doing before attending?

Community Management (glorified sales for a startup)

What is #1 reason you would recommend your school to a friend?

The community is rallying around Hackbright, so it is more than a technical education. You also get a lot of advice and help maneuvering through tech careers as a woman.

What programming languages did the (official) curriculum cover?

Python, Flask, SQLite, RegEx, JavaScript, Ruby (no Rails), HTML, CSS

Simon S., App Academy (San Francisco)

What is your favorite memory from the Program?

Ned the head instructor would sometimes stick around after class to demo the entire solution to a difficult project we were building that day. These were like movie nights, plus hundreds of "a-ha" moments.

Tell us a story around your decision to attend. What were your goals?

To surround myself with equally passionate people and to learn the most I could in a couple of months.

And why did you choose your particular school?

I was admitted to several similar programs. App Academy's deferred tuition option made more sense financially. I also liked the idea that my teachers would be so strongly incentivized to get me to the level I wanted to be at.

What were you doing before attending?

I was on the Obama campaign staff in Colorado.

What is the #1 reason you would recommend your school to a friend?

The other students. 50% of the learning comes from being surrounded by equally motivated and hard-working people.

What programming languages did the official curriculum cover?

Ruby & Ruby on Rails, JavaScript, CSS3/HTML5, SQL

Where do you now work and what is your role?

As a business staff at App Academy, San Francisco

Dave Melin, App Academy July 2013 (San Francisco)

What is your favorite memory from the Program?

Going to lunch with my fellow students and talking about the current projects and how everyone was going about their code.

Tell us a story around your decision to attend. What were your goals?

I was in finance doing accounting and felt like I needed to be in a career where I could contribute to the core product, while being more creative.

And why did you choose your particular school?

Only applied to one, but App Academy had great stats about their student success stories, and the tuition plan was unbeatable.

What were you doing before attending?

Accounting.

What is the #1 reason you would recommend your school to a friend?

The program is run by great people who genuinely want the students to be a successful and well educated developers.

What programming languages did the official curriculum cover?

Ruby & Ruby on Rails, JavaScript, SQL, CSS3/HTML5

Did you have a CS degree before attending?

No

Scott Rogers, App Academy 2013 (New York)

What is your favorite memory from the Program?

Demo days for the two capstone projects. I made weird apps, so it was pretty funny.

Tell us a story around your decision to attend. What were your goals?

I needed out of organic chemistry, because the field is insane. I wanted to become a capable developer who had the solid foundation necessary to become capable of teaching himself new technologies.

And why did you choose your particular school?

App Academy was the only one I got into. I interviewed Flatiron School and Launch Academy in Boston, but App Academy was my top choice due to finances.

What is the #1 reason you would recommend your school to a friend?

You will learn more than ever, and you will harder than ever, with classmates and instructors that really want you to succeed.

Where do you now work and what is your role?

Amplify Education, Software Engineer

Did you have a CS degree before attending?

No

Travis Sorensen, Codesmith (Los Angeles)

School website - https://www.codesmith.io/

What is your favorite memory from the Program?

When I finally understood React.js.

I had been struggling with this for about a week and was getting really frustrated with the pair programming learning style. I just wanted to the answer! The instructors kept using the Socratic Method (a case discussion with question prompts by the instructor) to nudge me in the right direction and I finally got it!

What made you choose this program? Why should someone attend this program?

I was looking for a program that was developed by both coders and educators.

What did the program do for you? What goals did it help you accomplish?

I can code! I'm looking to start my own business, but the job offers are pretty tempting.

Any word of advice for a prospective student?

Codesmith is an amazing learning experience. I stay late every night because I love it!

However, you're going to need to learn a fair amount of coding on your own before you can be accepted. Learning on your own through something like Codeschool is boring and you're going to think, "coding must just not be for me."

Power through it, coding is amazing and learning through pair programming is even better!

Chapter 7 Summary

- If you would like to share your story, please complete this brief survey (http://goo.gl/j4ybAF). You'll help others make a better decision!

8. Career Success Tips

You likely are joining a coding bootcamp with the intent of working in a software engineering career. (Not everyone does. I remember meeting Andrew, who told me that attending the bootcamp was his sabbatical. He just wanted to learn to program and build web products.)

You likely are thinking ahead about your dream companies, what kind of team you want to join, how to interview successfully, how to have a fun and successful career. For some, a career means a job at a growing company where you will have bundles of opportunities to learn and grow. Many bootcamp staff will tell you that you should often optimize for learning early on in your career. Knowledge is power, and you will be able to secure better-paying jobs if you focus on building your skills as a software engineer.

Others think of becoming a startup founder when they think of career success. For people like this, a program like the Viking Code School (VCS) may be an effective choice. VCS uses programming as a means to an end of building a web product, a baseline skill for many founders in the tech space.

It depends on your goals. If your dream is to open a clothing store, perhaps you should focus on studying fashion rather than programming. You can always hire a programmer. Context is also important. Suppose you are building a clothing store, but online. If you live in San Francisco, you likely can pair up with a technical co-founder. If you live in South Carolina, you might have to make a different choice.

Whatever the case may be, think about the context. What are your surroundings and what resources do you have at your disposal. Then, start with an end in mind. That is, have a specific goal so you can map out your path. Finally, focus on your strengths. If your plan is to be the sales leader for your organization, then learning programming just to know enough to be dangerous may end up being a waste of time.

Since you likely have specific questions on mind rather than seeking general success principles, I'll try to address a few commonly asked questions.

Do I need a CS degree?

Nope. It doesn't hurt, but you don't need one. I saw plenty of graduates get six figure jobs with no prior programming knowledge, let alone a degree. Some companies require a CS degree as a baseline. If you really must work at one of those companies, then it might be difficult to work there without a degree. But, it is possible. You just have to know the right people to get in the door.

What do employers want?

Employers are people just like you and me. If you remove the layer of abstraction, then it is just another human being reviewing your qualifications for a job they need done.

At a very generic level, employers want the same thing that the coding bootcamps wanted. Good people who learn quickly, work hard, and are fun to be around. At a more specific level, employers need a specific work done. If you can look beneath a job description and understand what the hiring manager needs, then you have a huge advantage. If you happen to know the hiring manager, and know what stresses her day to day, then you have a roadmap for crafting your pitch.

Of course, you need to pass the baseline knowledge tests and know your algorithms and data structures (still common in the industry). Beyond that, your customized pitch will win the day for you.

One last item on this question is that most employers don't really care what coding bootcamp you went to. If you have work experience, you'll already know this. Your employer probably didn't care much about what school you went to or what you majored in beyond interviews. Once the job started, your team only cared whether you could do the job.

And that's the powerful insight here. Regardless of your background, if you can demonstrate you can do the job, then you're more than half way there.

What about networking?

For some it's optional. If you happen to write a widely forked library, or wrote a best-selling technical book, then I think your work can speak for itself. Some people choose to take this route and focus on building something outstanding.

For others, networking is a must. Again, let's remove the abstraction from the word and think of this simply as getting to know someone. You wouldn't want to marry someone without ever meeting that person, would you? You wouldn't want to star drive in a car with a total stranger, would you? Well, think of networking as just meeting someone and getting to know personal things about that individual. As I noted above, if you personally get to know people and what they care about, you are on the fast lane in terms of job search.

Don't use networking as a crutch. You have to have the baseline skill. The talent market is competitive. Then again, you knew that right? That's why you're thinking about a coding bootcamp.

How do I find the right team?

Ah, the million dollar question that you forget to thinks about. When you are looking for a job, you tend to agonize over external attributes. You think about compensation and look at salary surveys. You want to know if your startup recently took in a big round of funding. You're curious about the stock options for employees.

But, come day one, you realize you are bored at your desk. What have you done?

Unless you have many mouths to feed and HAVE to optimize for earnings, I challenge you to think deeply about what you want. What kind of people do you work best with? Who can teach you the most? And what makes you happy? Do you see elements of what makes you better in the team that you will work with?

You know what they say. You are a product of the five people you spend most time around.

Think about that.

How do I position myself?

See above about networking and what employers want.

Pro Tips

Start with the end in mind - One of the most effective things you can do is to know where you are going. Sure that coding bootcamp is a guided path to your programming career. But, no one can tell you what your dream company or dream job is. Once you know what that looks like, you can focus on learning the skills that will get you there.

It's about them, not you - When you reach out to someone you don't know, make sure you do some research to make it about them, and not about you. For example, if you say something like "I want to learn more about your company," the subject is you. Reframe that to say "I think your

company is great and not enough people know about it."
Just an example.

What Are the Next Steps?

If there are tech shops you love, start networking today.
Find some folks who work there through different sources,
and reach out. For those who intend to be far away from a
tech center, don't despair. More and more developers are
doing work remotely.

Check out the following remote job sites:

- We Work Remotely
- We Work Meteor
- Or subscribe to the http://remoteok.io/ newsletter

Further, there are tools that do the shopping around of your
resume and qualifications for you. Check these out for
starters.

- underdog.io
- Hired

Further reading

If you have more time, the following articles about job search and interviewing are informative and revealing.

- Developers Guide to Interviewing on VentureBeat
- The Terrible Technical Interview on Techcrunch
- Cracking the Coding Interview video by Gayle Laakmann McDowell
- Lessons from a year's worth of hiring data by Aline Lerner

Chapter 8 Summary

- Job search and career preparation is a whole separate beast, so don't worry too much. One step at a time.
- Having an end in mind (where you want to be after bootcamp) will help you be more successful in the program and beyond.

9. Should You Move?

You might be wondering, does geography matter at all?

Jeff Casimir, director at Turing School shared his views about the advantages of attending a programming course in San Francisco Bay Area. (Turing School is based in Denver, Colorado.)

> *I'm obviously biased, but will give you a quick answer anyways:*
>
> *Not being in the SF ecosystem has plusses and minuses. On the downside, if you're in SF, you're a little minnow in a giant pool. Your cost of living during the program is super high. People probably haven't heard of the program you're in.*
>
> *On the other hand, they're craving developers. You can't turn around in the coffee shop without bumping into someone hiring. You can easily interview in person rather than scheduling trips or doing it over Skype.*

Being anywhere EXCEPT SF has minuses, too. Here in Denver there are dozens of jobs, not hundreds. Being here you're not totally immersed in the tech culture - people are more likely to talk about mountain biking than slinging code.

On the upside, there are way more job here than our students will fill up. I expect about 12 of our 23 students to stay in Colorado. You're a small fish in a small pond - people have heard of our program, they've been to our office -- essentially our program is the most interesting thing going on in Denver tech. Outside of Colorado, people are coming from SF, Seattle, Portland, NYC, etc to interview and (hopefully) hire our students.

Long story short: I don't think it matters. Pick a program that fits you and has people you like, the job part is easy.

It is an interesting insight.

My personal opinion is that location matters a lot. It matters, because context matters. Recall Kevin's story I shared in the introduction. Kevin began to learn on his own. However, he found learning on his own rather difficult. He ultimately decided to enroll in Dev Bootcamp San Francisco. There was nothing wrong with Kevin. No man is an island, and the best learning happens in best learning environments.

Location also has a big professional impact, even in this modern age of GitHub and Google Hangout. Many attend coding bootcamps with the intent of finding a job in software. Geography matters, because location (e.g. San Francisco) directly impacts 1) quantity of jobs, 2) quality of jobs, 3) compensation range, 4) community of like-minded peers, and 5) density of industry experts from whom you can learn more. Each factor is important, and the combined impact more so.

Again, I am quite biased in thinking that San Francisco is a great place to attend a full time programming course.

In reality, I imagine any dense tech center will give you similar benefits in your career. Based on reports of friends, cities like London, New York, Seattle, and Berlin support a healthy tech startup ecosystem.

Chapter 9 Summary

- There's nothing wrong with staying where you are. You will find great opportunities wherever you are.
- More and more developer work is done remotely.
- That said, there are awesome learning and career advantages to living in tech center.

P.S.

If you loved this book, please give a shout out on Amazon.com with a book review to let others know how this book helped you.

If you hated this book, please write me and let me know how I could make it better codingbootcamps@gmail.com. If you truly thought this book was worthless, I will give you your money back. At least let me know what the problem was and give me a chance to make it right.

Either way, your feedback will help me produce better books for you next time. So, please help.

If this guide helps you, consider giving back. Please pay it forward by completing this brief survey about your bootcamp experience.

Survey link – http://goo.gl/j4ybAF

About the Author

David failed at many businesses and careers and succeeded in some. He wants to help you avoid his mistakes. He wants you to be successful. He finds life fascinating and wants to learn many things.

He has consulted for Hack Reactor and Code School. He has curated Silicon Valley Startup Digest.

David writes at BetterAndHigher.com about his personal journey and working to be better in life. He tweets @findinbay.

You can also connect with David on StackOverflow or ask him questions on Quora.

Appendix 1: Applications Checklist

The application process will not be linear. So, please note that this is simply a reference point, and not a formula for success.

Invest in your own list of key factors for making your decision. Nevertheless, let me offer the following list to get you started. You may want to request some of the following information from programming course staff.

About the School

1. What are the standards of admission?
2. Describe the culture of the learning environment?
3. Can you describe the teaching philosophy? (e.g. how should students learn, do we pair?)
4. How large is the class size?
5. Who are my peers? With what sort of people will I be learning?
6. Can you refer me to an alumni who can share his or her experience?
7. What are the payment options? Is a deferred payment option available?

8. What makes your programming course unique (or better or special) from others?

9. Can you tell me about the employment statistics? What are the median salaries? Who are the employers? What is the graduate placement rate? (Remember, geographic location is a key driver behind these questions.)

10. Do you offer employment help in the form of coaching or networking?

11. Can you share some details about the curriculum? Basically, what can I expect to learn?

12. Tell me about the instructors. What is their pedigree (companies where they worked)?

13. What is the instructor to student ratio?

You will also want to dig online to assess the reputation of the programming course. Resources include Quora, Reddit, Hacker News, YouTube Channels, and alumni blogs.

Finally, answer for yourself these important questions. These are unique and personal to you. As you answer these questions, be true to yourself. Only you can be you.

About Yourself

- How will learning to code help me? Am I interested simply because it is cool, or because I want to work as a software engineer? (Do I understand that working as a software engineer could mean staying up late night tracking down someone else's bug?)

- Have I asked a senior software engineer at a company that I am interested in working for what they think of this development path? Basically, what is my post-course game plan?

- Does the curriculum align with the job skill-set that I want to gain? For example, is the school's key programming language consistent with jobs I'd like to have?

- Your own gut check. Step back. Does it feel right? If not, why not? (Again, be you. Only you can be you. Don't do it just because you saw someone else do it and they seem happy.)

Appendix 2: Books and Other Resources

The following is a super brief, but super useful list of links and learning resources to help you with your next steps.

Online Directories

There are definitely dozens of online lists of bootcamps, but here are a few that stand out.

switchup

Course Report

BootCamper

Additionally, Kapor Center's list and this Quora post deserve a mention.

Kapor Center Coding Nation List

Quora Best Bootcamps in US

Freebies!

Good books are priceless as learning tools. I want to share some of them with you.

Don't (over)pay for your coding books, if you don't mind reading it electronically. You'll save a bundle with this resource!

IT eBooks

The books here aren't linked to any affiliate codes. It's just free. Browse for and download awesome books to your heart's content!

You're welcome!

Books are great! Sometimes, though, you just need something lighter in your inbox. What newsletters should you subscribe to?

If you go to Cooper Press, you'll find lots of awesome weekly tech newsletters. For example, you might like the JavaScript Weekly and Ruby Weekly if you are getting ready for a coding bootcamp. There are more, so check them out judiciously. Don't overdo it, since your mental bandwidth will be limited.

I also want to recommend some stellar books that can complement your education. These are some stand-outs among dozens and dozens of books. Otherwise, you're going to get trigger happy and burn a lot of time on lot of programming books. Hopefully, this will save you some time as you start out.

> *In full disclosure, some of the links in the following sections contain affiliate codes. That means for a purchase, a small part of the proceeds will come to me. I hope you don't mind that. You will not be paying any more than you would otherwise; the affiliate fee comes directly from the author royalties. The proceeds help me keep the cost of the book low for readers. I wanted to let you know in advance. Thanks for your trust and understanding.*

For Ruby and Ruby on Rails Trek:

Code School $9 first month introductory offer (normally it is $29 per month). Or sign-up for an annual account. (Print readers can use link - http://mbsy.co/7QR8Q - for $9 first month trial.)

For JavaScript, Angular, Meteor Trek:

- The Node Beginner Handbook by Manuel Kiessling
- MEAN Machine by Chris Sevilleja and Holly Lloyd (MEAN stands for MongoDB, Express, Angjularjs, and Node.)

Productivity, Tools, and Personal Development

As a professional software engineer, good tools and work environment will be key part of your success. This means choosing and learning text editors and source code management tools.

You may be fond of Emacs or Vim familiar from the Unix world. That said, modern text editors like Sublime or textmate are in many ways revolutionary. Here are some books to help you learn more about your text editor of choice.

- Sublime Productivity by Josh Earl

- Trello Dojo by Daniel Root - Trello is a super simple task board and is well-suited to building simple software projects.
- Fifty Quick Ideas to Improve your User Stories by Gojko Adzic and David Evans
- How to Do What You Love & Earn What You're Worth as a Programmer by Raganwald
- What I've Learned From Failure by Raganwald

Algorithms Practice

- Code Wars - programming challenges and katas
- Interview Cake - a tool built by a friend, Parker
- Coderwall - a crowd-sourced site, Assembly-made

www.ingramcontent.com/pod-product-compliance
Lightning Source LLC
Chambersburg PA
CBHW051208050326
40689CB00008B/1241